NATIONAL AUDUBON SOCIETY

Gardener's Journal

Pomegranate

Audubon

Audubon

The Audubon mission is to conserve and restore natural ecosystems, focusing on birds, other wildlife, and their habitats for the benefit of humanity and the earth's biological diversity.

Through its education, science, and public policy initiatives, Audubon engages people throughout the US and Latin America in conservation. Audubon's Centers and its sanctuaries and education programs are developing the next generation of conservation leaders by providing opportunities for families, students, teachers, and others to learn about and enjoy the natural world. The science program is focused on connecting people with nature through projects like Audubon At Home and Great Backyard Bird Count. Audubon's volunteer Citizen Scientists participate in research and conservation action in a variety of ways, from monitoring bird populations and restoring critical wildlife habitat to implementing healthy habitat practices in their own backyards. Audubon's public policy programs are supported by a strong foundation of science, environmental education, and grassroots engagement. With its network of state offices, chapters, and volunteers, Audubon works to protect and restore our natural heritage.

To learn how you can support Audubon, call (800) 274-4201, visit www.audubon.org, or write to Audubon, 700 Broadway, New York NY 10003.

The Audubon At Home program is supported in part by funds from the US Department of Agriculture's Natural Resources Conservation Service (www.nrcs.usda.gov).

Designed by Lisa Reid
Printed in China on recycled paper

Published by Pomegranate Communications, Inc.
Box 808022, Petaluma CA 94975
800 227 1428; www.pomegranate.com

Pomegranate Europe Ltd.
Unit 1, Heathcote Business Centre, Hurlbutt Road
Warwick, Warwickshire CV34 6TD, UK
[+44] 0 1926 430111; sales@pomeurope.co.uk

Catalog No. AA310
ISBN 0-7649-3317-5

14 13 12 11 10 09 08 07 06 05   10 9 8 7 6 5 4 3 2 1

Contents

Introduction 4

Attracting Birds and Butterflies 5

Healthy Garden Design 9

Bird Habitat Necessities 14

Bird-Feeding Basics 19

List of Paintings 23

The Twelve Months

    January 27

    February 39

    March 51

    April 63

    May 75

    June 87

    July 99

    August 111

    September 123

    October 135

    November 147

    December 159

Resources 170

Appendix I: Take Action! Plant Natives .172

Appendix II: Take Action! Protect Water Quality 175

Appendix III: Take Action! Reduce Pesticide Use 178

Suppliers 183

Plant List 187

USDA Plant Hardiness Zone Map 191

Audubon Membership 192

The *Audubon Gardener's Journal* is designed to help you plan and monitor your garden week by week throughout the year, and to encourage you to create healthy gardens and yards that will attract and protect birds, butterflies, and other wildlife. By planting native species and providing water sources, food, and shelter, you will be on your way to enjoying a beautiful and robust garden with your avian neighbors.

The beginning sections of this journal offer suggestions for planning and creating your garden. Several pages of graph-lined paper follow (for plotting out your garden design), and then the twelve monthly sections begin. Each month's introduction offers tips and reminders of things to do that month; each weekly double-page spread offers space for you to record your notes, observations, and sketches.

The journal ends with lists of resources, appendixes about important ways to promote ecologically sound gardens, directory pages for you to list your favorite suppliers, and plant list pages for you to record your observations about plants you've grown, tried to grow, or hope to grow.

Filled with John James Audubon's glorious illustrations of birds, this journal will be not only an invaluable tool and resource, but also, we hope, a pleasure to use. Happy gardening!

Plants for Common Birds

They are like old friends: the familiar birds that traverse through your yard or visit your feeder almost every day. Robins, cardinals, goldfinches, jays, juncos, and many other abundant species are some of America's common garden birds.

Birds rely on the resources that nature provides, often plants that supply them with fruits, nuts, and an array of insects. Plants also provide shelter and nesting sites along with nest material, perches from which to survey, and safe places to sleep or wait out a storm.

Using native plants in your backyard landscape will offer the most resources to birds and serve as rewarding attractants. Science has proven that certain birds prefer the foods and resources offered by particular native plants with which they may have coevolved. This provides a logical and simple solution to the question of how to help common species: plant the plants that birds use. Plant a variety of species to mimic natural habitat. (See Appendix I in this journal for more information about planting native species.)

Here are a few regional suggestions for some of your favorite birds:

Northeast

Highbush blueberry (*Vaccinium corymbosum*) (shrub) attracts thirty species of birds including American robin, eastern bluebird, scarlet tanager, eastern and spotted towhees, gray catbird, northern mockingbird, brown thrasher, and northern cardinal.

Common serviceberry (*Amelanchier arborea*) (shrub/small tree) bears sweet-tasting fruits that many birds find irresistible, including wood thrush, rose-breasted grosbeak, eastern bluebird, and red-eyed vireo.

Eastern red cedar *(Juniperus virginiana)* (tree) attracts many birds, including cedar waxwing, northern mockingbird, brown thrasher, gray catbird, ruffed grouse, American robin, mourning dove, purple finch, common crow, northern flicker, downy woodpecker, evening grosbeak, yellow-bellied sapsucker, and eastern bluebird.

Bearberry *(Arctostaphylos uva-ursi)* (groundcover) provides cover and berries to fox sparrow, grouse, and other species.

Southeast

Southern magnolia *(Magnolia grandiflora)* (tree) attracts eastern kingbird, northern mockingbird, northern flicker, red-bellied woodpecker, and wood thrush, among other species.

Sassafras *(Sassafras albidum)* (tree) bears blue fruits favored by over twenty species, including eastern kingbird, gray catbird, eastern bluebird, and pileated woodpecker.

Arrowwood viburnum *(Viburnum dentatum)* (shrub) attracts eastern bluebird, northern flicker, gray catbird, American robin, and other birds.

Virginia creeper *(Parthenocissus quinquefolia)* (vine) attracts various species of woodpecker, vireo, thrush, and warbler as well as eastern bluebird.

Central Plains and Prairies

Big bluestem *(Andropogon gerardii)* (graminoid/grass) provides cover for at least twenty-four species of songbirds and nesting sites or seeds for Grasshopper, Henslow's, and other sparrows as well as nesting sites for sedge wren and western meadowlark.

Gray dogwood *(Cornus racemosa)* (tree) is used by many species, including northern cardinal, downy woodpecker, northern flicker, and eastern bluebird.

Sargent crabapple *(Malus sargentii)* (tree) attracts gray catbird, cedar waxwing, American robin, and evening grosbeak, among others.

Flameleaf sumac *(Rhus copallina)* (shrub) bears fruits that appeal to many birds, including pileated woodpecker, northern flicker, red-winged blackbird, and American robin.

Western Mountains and Deserts

Honey mesquite *(Prosopis glandulosa var. Torr.)* (tree) attracts species that include curve-billed thrasher, Gambel's quail, and white-winged dove.

Rocky Mountain juniper *(Juniperus scopulorum)* (shrub) attracts cedar waxwing, northern mockingbird, evening grosbeak, and other birds.

Firethorn *(Pyracantha coccinea)* (shrub) provides winter cover and berries that are eaten by at least seventeen species, including Bohemian and cedar waxwing, American robin, and northern mockingbird.

Bunchberry *(Cornus canadensis)* (groundcover) attracts small foraging birds such as vireos.

Pacific Coast

California wax myrtle *(Myrica californica)* (shrub) lures northern flicker, chestnut-backed chickadee, yellow-rumped warbler, tree swallow, California towhee, and spotted towhee, among others.

Lantana *(Lantana spp.)* (shrub/ground cover) is a versatile plant attractive to western bluebird, ash-throated flycatcher, western kingbird, yellow-breasted chat, and lazuli bunting.

California live oak *(Quercus agrifolia)* (tree) attracts oak titmouse, western scrub jay, Steller's jay, chestnut-backed chickadee, and about thirty other species of birds.

Toyon *(Heteromeles arbutifolia)* (tree), also known as California holly, has red berries eaten by many species, including American robin, hermit thrush, wrentit, northern flicker, northern mockingbird, cedar waxwing, and western bluebird.

Bird-Attracting Flowers

Aster (*Aster* spp.)

Bachelor's button (*Centaurea hirta*)

Basket flower (*Centaurea americana*)

Bellflower (*Campanula* spp.)

Black-eyed Susan (*Rudbeckia* spp.)

Blessed thistle (*Carduus benedictus*)

Calendula (*Calendula officinalis*)

California poppy (*Eschscholzia californica*)

China aster (*Callistephus chinensis*)

Chrysanthemum (*Chrysanthemum* spp.)

Coreopsis (*Coreopsis* spp.)

Cornflower (*Centaurea cyanus*)

Cosmos (*Cosmos* spp.)

Crested cockscomb (*Celosia cristata*)

Dayflower (*Commelina* spp.)

Dusty miller (*Centaurea cineraria*)

Love-lies-bleeding (*Amaranthus caudatus*)

Phlox (*Phlox* spp.), especially *P. drummondii*

Portulaca (*Portulaca* spp.), especially moss rose (*P. grandiflora*)

Prince's plume (*Celosia plumosa*)

Rock purslane (*Calandrinia* spp.)

Royal sweet sultan (*Centaurea imperialis*)

Silene (*Silene* spp.)

Sunflower (*Helianthus annuus*)

Sweet scabious (*Scabiosa atropurpurea*)

Tarweed (*Madia elegans*)

Verbena (*Verbena hybrida*)

Zinnia (*Zinnia elegans*)

Lists on pages 8 and 9 reprinted from *National Audubon Society: The Bird Garden*, by Stephen W. Kress. Text © 1995 Stephen W. Kress. Reprinted by permission of DK Publishing. All rights reserved.

Plants for Hummingbirds

Bee balm/Oswego tea *(Monarda didyma)*; perennial herb

Butterfly bush *(Buddleia davidii)*; shrub

Canada columbine *(Aquilegia canadensis)*; perennial herb

Cardinal flower *(Lobelia cardinalis)*; perennial herb

Citrus *(Citrus* spp.); tree

Coral bean *(Erythrina* spp.); tree

Coral bell *(Heuchera sanguinea)*; perennial herb

Four o'clock *(Mirabilis jalapa)*; perennial herb

Fuchsia *(Fuchsia* spp.); flowering shrub

Hibiscus *(Hibiscus* spp.); flowering shrub

Hollyhock *(Althea* spp.); perennial herb

Honeysuckle *(Lonicera dioica, L. ciliosa, L. sempervirens)*;
    flowering shrub/climbing vine

Indian paintbrush *(Castilleja* spp.); annual and perennial herb

Jewelweed *(Impatiens* spp.); annual herb

Larkspur *(Consolida ambigua)*; annual herb

Lemon bottlebrush *(Callistemon lanceolatus)*; shrub

Morning glory *(Ipomoea* spp.); annual vine

Penstemon *(Penstemon* spp.); perennial herb

Petunia *(Petunia* spp.); annual herb

Phlox *(Phlox drummondii* and spp.); annual and perennial herb

Salvia *(Salvia* spp.); annual and perennial herb

Scarlet runner bean *(Phaseolus coccineus)*; cultivated legume vine

Trumpet vine *(Campsis radicans)*; native vine

Weigela *(Weigela* spp.); flowering shrub

Zinnia *(Zinnia elegans)*; annual herb

For the latest list of plants for each North American region and the species that visit the plants, see the National Audubon Society's *North American Birdfeeder Guide,* by Robert Burton and Stephen W. Kress, New York: DK Publishing, 2005.

Healthy Garden Design

A healthy yard is not really a "yard" at all. It's a habitat, a sanctuary for wildlife and for you and your family. A healthy habitat provides a natural haven beneficial to birds, other creatures, and people, and is an extension of your home and part of a larger ecoregion. Learn how to be a responsible caretaker of your piece of the earth. In creating an outdoor space that's healthy for wildlife, for you and your family, and for the environment at large, start by keeping these basic principles in mind:

EMPHASIZE:
- Native Plants
- Water Features
- Food for Birds
- Nest Sites

MINIMIZE:
- Invasive Plants
- Turf Lawn
- Free-roaming Cats
- Impervious Surfaces

There is no single "ideal," no formula that says you must have so many of this and so much of that for your yard to be vital. You can mix and match to suit your tastes and desires. Though you'll be designing and planting your space with a purpose, there's room for imagination and fun. When you view your yard as habitat, your ecological awareness will be heightened. For instance, you'll begin looking at plants for their edible offerings: Do they bear fruit, nuts, seeds, nectar? Your yard will be practical but bountiful as well.

The objective is to increase food and water sources for wildlife, shelter and nesting opportunities, native plantings, and biodiversity while decreasing invasive plant sprawl, lawn size, water and pesticide use, and polluted runoff. As you change or introduce an element, ask "Who or what will benefit from this action?" and "How does it affect the environment beyond my home?"

Garden Basics

The success of a garden, whether large or small, depends on one basic idea: plants will thrive best if planted in the right spot, a location where the conditions of water, light, climate, and soil match those to which the plants are adapted. To ensure proper plant placement in the restoration and management of your backyard habitat, you'll need a plan.

Natural Design

Map out your property—using the graph paper in this journal is a handy way to do this—showing all elements of the area, such as the house, driveway, paths, stone walls, existing plants, lawn, etc. Note areas of sunlight and shade, wind direction, wet and dry spots, soil type, and soil pH. With tracing paper or clear acetate, create overlays to the map indicating areas that will be removed and those that will be added. You may want to involve a landscape designer, use landscape software, or visit the Audubon website for more ideas:
www.audubon.org/bird/at_home/HealthyYard_Create.html

Rethink Your Lawn

If each one of us who takes care of a lawn (49 million US households) replaced just ONE square yard (nine square feet) of lawn with alternative plantings, we would:

- Stop 60,000 tons of grass clippings from finding their way to a landfill
- Provide more than 10,000 acres of better habitat for wildlife
- Eliminate 1.2 million hours of mowing

For an action plan to transform your lawn, visit
www.audubon.org/bird/at_home/HealthyYard_GardenBasics.html#P51_1388

Growing Conditions

• Find the planting zone you live in on a USDA plant hardiness zone map (see map p. 191). This average temperature range will guide you in purchasing plants that can survive in your climate.

• Be aware of various microenvironments around your home, which create specialized growing conditions. For instance, a hillside may be more susceptible to wind, calling for tougher, drought-tolerant plants.

• Know the average rainfall in your area, and more specifically, recognize areas of your outdoor space that tend to be wet or dry most of the season. Plant accordingly.

Soil Compost

• Know the type, quality, and pH of your soil. Whether the soil is sand or clay, whether it has enough nutrients, and whether it is acidic or alkaline all make a difference to a plant. These elements determine water retention, food sources, and nutrient availability. A simple testing kit can give you pH readings, but for a complete soil profile, you'll need to send a sample to a lab. Contact your local Cooperative Extension for soil testing facilities in your area.

• Understand the soil needs for the plants you choose, matching plants with your soil type. For instance, native plants found in woodlands prefer rich soil, as is found on the forest floor. Other natives, such as those found in dry, exposed soils, prefer less fertile earth.

• If you find that your soil needs improving to increase its nutrient and moisture-holding capacities, add decayed organic matter such as compost. Compost is a remedy for many soil problems, and because healthy soil translates to healthy plants, the creation of a compost pile is a must for gardeners. In addition, it saves precious landfill space.

Light Considerations

• The south side of the house is the brightest, hottest, and driest, while the north side is darkest, least warm, and often wet.

• Determine the areas that get full sun, partial sun, and shade and mark these on your map. This will further help you select the correct plant for the site.

Regard for Wildlife

• Connect planting areas—from your front yard to back yard, and from your yard to your neighbors' yards—to create a wildlife corridor.

• Vary the levels of vegetation to mimic natural landscape structure and provide wildlife habitat. Plant large and small trees, shrubs, herbaceous undergrowth, groundcovers, and vines. Keep the tier idea even for meadows and wetlands, designing with plants of different heights.

• Plant in masses rather than an individual plant here and there: it's more aesthetically pleasing and much more valuable to wildlife.

• Retain dead trees and snags where safety permits to provide foraging, nesting, and perching opportunities for birds and other wildlife.

• Rake leaf litter under and in front of shrubs to provide a mulch cover for plants and foraging area for ground-feeding birds. In similar fashion, rake brush into piles that provide areas of shelter and protection for wildlife.

• Use natural borders rather than fencing. Mix a variety of native shrubs to create a hedgerow that is beneficial to wildlife, aesthetically pleasing, and maintenance-free.

Bird Habitat Necessities

The needs of birds aren't much different from our own. Food and water are absolute basics, but so is shelter or cover to serve as protection from the weather and a safe place to raise a family. Provide these fundamental elements in your backyard habitat, and you will attract numerous visitors.

Food

Many backyard birds are insect eaters, but will supplement their diet with nuts, seeds, fruit, or nectar, depending on the species. Increase the array of foods you offer, and you will increase the diversity of birds you will attract and support.

Natural sources: Nothing beats natural, native vegetation to feed the birds of your area, so plant a variety of native plants and in a combination that supplies food year-round. Following is a list to get you started. To learn more, visit "Plants for Birds and Wildlife" at the Audubon website (www.audubon.org). Also, as previously stated, the way you maintain your garden can supply additional food sources. For example, leaves raked into your garden bed and under shrubs can provide foraging areas for ground-feeding birds such as sparrows, juncos, thrashers, and robins.

Food Type	Natural Source	Birds Attracted
Nuts	Oak, hickory, buckeye, beech, walnut	Woodpeckers, nuthatches, jays, wild turkeys
Seeds	Pine, spruce, fir, maple, alder, sunflowers, coneflowers, asters, goldenrod, grasses	Woodpeckers, grosbeaks, finches, bobwhites, cardinals, pine siskins, chickadees, crossbills, jays, nuthatches, juncos, sparrows, wild turkeys, titmice, doves, blackbirds
Fruit	Holly, dogwood, serviceberry, cherry, elderberry, red Mulberry, hackberry, bayberry, raspberry, blueberry, high-bush cranberry, pokeberry, Virginia creeper, grape, cactus	Thrushes, veeries, robins, catbirds, cedar waxwings, mockingbirds, bluebirds, sparrows, woodpeckers, tanagers, juncos, grouse, thrashers, wrens, flickers, roadrunners, vireos, bobwhites, yellow-rumped warblers
Nectar	Various flowers, especially red tubular flowers, such as columbine, lobelia, penstemon, azalea, fuchsia, trumpet vine, bee balm, and native honeysuckle; also yucca	Hummingbirds, orioles

Supplemental sources: Millions of people enjoy feeding birds, and feeders can help birds in especially harsh winters. A feeding station with a variety of bird feeders suited to the eating habits of different species will attract the greatest number of species. For instance, some birds feed on the ground, others like perching; some prefer sunflower seeds, others millet, thistle, suet, or nectar.

Water

All birds need water for drinking and for bathing. By providing a clean, fresh source, you will attract more species than will visit bird feeders.

Natural sources: If you have a natural water source on your property, such as a stream or wetland, enhance its attractiveness and wildlife value by protecting and restoring native plant species and allowing the vegetation along the banks to grow high, to create a buffer zone.

Supplemental sources:

• Birdbaths. This is a simple, popular way to provide water, with endless designs available at garden centers and wild bird supply stores. The sides should incline gently to a depth of no more than two to three inches. The surface should be rough for better footing. To protect vulnerable bathing birds from lurking predators, locate the bath some distance from cover; about fifteen feet is a good distance. Change the water every few days and keep the bath scrubbed clean, but do not use detergents or bleach. Birds are attracted to the sound of running water, and a drip or misting feature will increase the number of visitors. Water heaters will keep the water free of ice during winter months in colder climates.

• Ponds and Water Gardens. The creation of these water elements will take some work, but, done well, they can attract many species. Ponds for birds should be shallow, with gently sloping shorelines.

See Appendix II in this journal for more information about protecting the quality of water in your yard and garden.

Nesting

Birds will remain in your habitat during the breeding season if they have places to nest and raise young. Different species have different requirements. Some nest in cavities, many others in open nests found on ledges or in a tree crotch, and others on the ground. Get to know which species are likely to nest in your area and provide the appropriate habitat or structure.

Natural sources: Native trees and shrubs provide good nesting areas for many species, from those that nest in holes to those that create cup-shaped nests in the crotches of branches to those that build nests at the tops of the canopy. Include a mix of evergreen and deciduous plants, a hedgerow, and vines. For grassland species such as meadowlarks, make sure you let a meadow grow all season, mowing only in late summer or early fall. Where safety permits, allow snags—dead trees—to remain standing. Woodpeckers and others excavate the rotting wood looking for insects; the resulting holes are used by cavity-nesting birds. Woodpeckers also require dead trees for drumming—their way of defending their nesting territory.

Supplemental sources: Nest boxes make a wonderful addition to a yard, allowing you to easily watch a family raise its young. Wrens, swallows, bluebirds, purple martins, chickadees, and titmice are some of the species that readily use nest boxes. Identify the species of bird you'd like to attract to determine the correct size of the entrance hole needed. You may want to consider erecting a shelf-style structure for species such as robins and phoebes. Nest boxes should be mounted on a pole, fence post, or tree. Height of the nest depends on the species. For most backyard cavity nesters, a height of at least five feet is recommended. Location is also important, as each species has a preferred habitat. Bluebirds, for example, prefer open fields. If a bluebird house is located too close to human housing, house sparrows may take the box; house wrens may occupy the box if it is located too close to shrubs. In northern latitudes, it is best to face boxes with entrances to the east to provide morning warmth. This guideline is less important in southern latitudes.

Ventilation and drainage holes are necessary, as is access to the interior to allow annual fall and spring cleaning. Baffles and other guards to deter climbing predators such as raccoons and snakes are encouraged. You can assist birds in building their nests by supplying some of the materials they seek, such as twigs; short lengths of string, yarn, and thread; cotton; hair brushed from a pet; and sphagnum moss. Provide the offerings in a tray or in an onion net bag hung from a tree.

Shelter

Birds need places where they can hide from predators and inclement weather. Trees, shrubs, meadows, and even rock walls provide such shelter.

Natural sources: Native trees and shrubs of different densities and heights give birds places of retreat and safety. In winter, evergreens, hedgerows, and dense thickets offer critical cover. Place feeding stations close enough to vegetation so that birds can make a quick escape but far enough to allow for a wide visual field for watching possible threats.

Supplemental sources: A dry stone wall, with its nooks and crannies, or simply small piles of rocks can provide hiding spots, as can a pile of logs. You can also erect boxes designed specifically for roosting, with the entrance hole near the bottom so that heat doesn't escape. Mount the box in a sheltered area, preferably facing south.

Over one hundred North American bird species supplement their natural diets with bird seed, suet, fruit, and nectar obtained from feeders. Bird feeding can benefit birds and also provide great bird watching from your own backyard. The obvious time to feed birds is in winter, when natural food supplies are scarce; however, additional species visit feeders during the spring and fall migrations, and also during summer while nesting.

To keep birds coming back to your feeders in any season, provide them with the following three essential elements:

- A variety of quality seed.

- Fresh water for drinking and bathing.

- Ample cover, preferably provided by native plants. Native plants also provide potential nesting sites and a source of natural food.

Keep in mind that bird feeders also present potential risks, such as window collisions, predation, and exposure to disease. Following are some topics and tips for safely attracting and feeding birds.

Locate feeders at different levels. Sparrows, juncos, and towhees usually feed on the ground, while finches and cardinals feed in shrubs, and chickadees, titmice, and woodpeckers feed in trees. To avoid crowding and to attract the greatest variety of species, provide tablelike feeders for ground-feeding birds, hopper or tube feeders for shrub and treetop feeders, and suet feeders well off the ground for woodpeckers, nuthatches, and chickadees.

Offer a variety of seeds in separate feeders. A variety of seeds will attract the greatest variety of birds. To avoid waste, offer different seeds in different feeders, such as sunflower seeds, nyger (thistle) seeds, and peanuts. Black oil sunflower seed appeals to the greatest number of birds. When using blends, choose mixtures containing sunflower seeds, millet, and cracked corn—the three most popular types of bird seed. Birds that are sunflower specialists will readily eat the sunflower seed and toss the millet and corn to the ground, to be eaten by ground-feeding birds such as sparrows and juncos. Mixtures of peanuts, nuts, and dried fruit are attractive to woodpeckers, nuthatches, and titmice. Relatively few species prefer milo, wheat, and oats, which are featured in less expensive blends.

Provide suet during cool weather only. Suet (beef fat) attracts insect-eating birds such as woodpeckers, wrens, chickadees, nuthatches, and titmice. Place the suet in special feeders or net onion bags at least five feet from the ground to keep it out of the reach of dogs. Do not put out suet during hot weather, as it can turn rancid; also, dripping fat can damage natural waterproofing on bird feathers.

Peanut butter pudding is a good substitute for suet in the summer. Mix one part peanut butter with five parts corn meal and stuff the mixture into holes drilled in a hanging log or into the crevices of a large pinecone. This all-season mixture attracts woodpeckers, chickadees, titmice, and occasionally warblers.

Fruit for berry-eating birds: Fruit specialists such as robins, waxwings, bluebirds, and mockingbirds rarely eat bird seed. To attract these birds, soak raisins and currants in water overnight, then place them on a table feeder, or purchase blends with a dried fruit mixture. To attract orioles and tanagers, skewer halved oranges onto a spike near other feeders, or provide nectar feeders.

Nectar for hummingbirds: Make a sugar solution of one part white sugar to four parts water. Boil briefly to sterilize and dissolve sugar crystals; no need to add red food coloring. Feeders must be washed every few days with very hot water and kept scrupulously clean to prevent the growth of mold.

Protect birds from window collisions. In the United States, approximately one billion birds die from flying into windows each year. Protect birds from collisions by placing feeders within three feet of windows, if possible. Mobiles and opaque decorations hanging outside windows help to prevent bird strikes, or attach fruit tree netting outside windows to deflect birds from the glass.

Store seed in secure metal containers, such as metal garbage cans with secure lids, to protect it from squirrels and mice. Keep the cans in a cool, dry location; avoid storing in the heat. Damp seeds may grow mold that can be fatal to birds. Overheating can destroy the nutrition and taste of sunflower seeds. For these reasons, it's best not to keep seed from one winter to the next.

Discourage squirrels from consuming feeder foods. Squirrels are best excluded by placing feeders on a pole in an open area. Pole-mounted feeders should be about five feet off the ground and protected by a cone-shaped baffle (at least seventeen inches in diameter) or similar obstacle below the feeder. Locate pole-mounted feeders at least ten feet from the nearest shrub, tree, or other tall structure.

Keep cats indoors. Cats kill hundreds of millions of birds annually in the United States, often pouncing on ground-feeding birds and those dazed by window collisions. Responsible and caring cat owners keep their cats indoors, where they are also safer from traffic, disease, and fights with other animals. Outdoor cats are especially dangerous to birds in the spring, when fledglings are on the ground. Bells on cat collars are usually ineffective for deterring predation.

Clean feeders and rake up spilled grain and hulls. Uneaten seed can become soggy and grow deadly mold. Empty and clean feeders twice a year (spring and fall), more often if feeders are used during humid summers. Using a long-handled bottlebrush, scrub with dish detergent and rinse with a powerful hose; then soak in a bucket of 10 percent non-chlorine bleach solution, rinse well, and dry in the sun. In early spring, rake up spilled grain and sunflower hulls.

John James Audubon's Paintings

John James Audubon's bird paintings reproduced in this journal are from *Audubon's Birds of America.*

Cover   *Anna's Hummingbird [Columbian Humming Bird]* (detail)

1   *Anna's Hummingbird [Columbian Humming Bird]* (detail)

4   *Anna's Hummingbird [Columbian Humming Bird]* (detail)

9   *Ruby-throated Hummingbird [Ruby-throated Humming Bird]* (detail)

14   *Eastern Bluebird [Blue-bird]* (detail)

26   *Common Yellowthroat [Roscoe's Yellow-throat]* (detail)

27   *Grasshopper Sparrow [Yellow-winged Sparrow]* (detail)

38   *Common Flicker [Golden-winged Woodpecker]*

39   *Carolina Wren [Great Carolina Wren]*

50–51   *Eastern Bluebird [Blue-bird]* (details)

62   *Warbling Vireo [Warbling Flycatcher]*

63   *Nashville Warbler*

74   *Hooded Warbler [Selby's Flycatcher]* (detail)

86–87   *Blue-winged Warbler [Blue-winged Yellow Warbler]* (details)

98   *Painted Bunting* (detail)

99   *Palm Warbler [Yellow Red-poll Warbler]* (detail)

110   *Carolina Chickadee [Black-capped Titmouse]* (detail)

111   *Wood Thrush* (detail)

122   *Say's Phoebe [Say's Flycatcher], Western Kingbird [Arkansaw Flycatcher], Scissor-tailed Flycatcher [Swallow-tailed Flycatcher]* (detail)

134   *Wood Thrush* (detail)

146–147   *Western Tanager [Louisiana Tanager], Scarlet Tanager [Black-winged Red-bird]* (details)

158   *Scrub Jay [Ultramarine Jay], Steller's Jay, Yellow-billed Magpie, Clark's Nutcracker [Clark's Crow]* (detail)

159   *Cedar Waxwing [Cedar Bird]* (detail)

171   *Least Bittern* (detail)

Back Cover   *Northern Parula Warbler [Blue Yellow-back Warbler]* (detail)

General Thoughts, Observations, & Sketches

TIPS AND REMINDERS

THE TIMING FOR THESE EVENTS WILL DEPEND ON LATITUDE.

- Take note of which areas birds are using for winter shelter and foraging so that you will be sure to preserve them. Also make note of any areas that could benefit from additional vegetation.

- Have fun perusing seed and nursery catalogs and placing your orders. Refer to the notes, photographs, and sketches you made during the summer to determine the types and quantities of plants needed to boost your backyard habitat.

- To gain traction on ice or snow, use sand or sawdust from untreated wood, materials that are less harmful to plants than salt.

January

General Thoughts, Observations, & Sketches

General Thoughts, Observations, & Sketches

January
WEEK 1

Weather • Hours of Sun _____

_____

_____

_____

In Bloom _____

_____

_____

_____

Plant Notes _____

_____

_____

_____

Tree Notes _____

_____

_____

_____

Yard Notes _____

_____

_____

_____

Visitors _____

_____

_____

January
WEEK 2

Weather • Hours of Sun _____

_____

_____

_____

_____

In Bloom _____

_____

_____

_____

Plant Notes _____

_____

_____

_____

Tree Notes _____

_____

_____

_____

_____

Yard Notes _____

_____

_____

_____

Visitors _____

_____

_____

_____

General Thoughts, Observations, & Sketches WEEK 2

January
WEEK 3

Weather • Hours of Sun _____

_____

_____

_____

In Bloom _____

_____

_____

_____

Plant Notes _____

_____

_____

_____

Tree Notes _____

_____

_____

_____

Yard Notes _____

_____

_____

_____

Visitors _____

_____

_____

January
WEEK 4

Weather • Hours of Sun

_____

_____

_____

_____

In Bloom

_____

_____

_____

Plant Notes

_____

_____

_____

_____

Tree Notes

_____

_____

_____

_____

Yard Notes

_____

_____

_____

Visitors

_____

_____

_____

THE TIMING FOR THESE EVENTS WILL DEPEND ON LATITUDE.

- Participate in the Great Backyard Bird Count
  www.birdsource.org/gbbc/

- Take advantage of the time spent indoors to learn about the environment connected to your backyard habitat. Research your ecological address.

- Read about the harmful effects of various herbicides, insecticides, and fertilizers; explore alternatives to pesticides; and review best practices for your lawn and garden.

- Collect the wood ashes from your fireplace to use in your compost pile or to sift and add with sand and loam to create a dust bath for birds in summer.

- Sharpen and tune-up your garden tools for the season ahead.

February

General Thoughts, Observations, & Sketches

February

WEEK 1

Weather • Hours of Sun

_____

In Bloom

_____

Plant Notes

_____

Tree Notes

_____

Yard Notes

_____

Visitors

_____

February
WEEK 2

Weather • Hours of Sun _____

_____

_____

_____

In Bloom _____

_____

_____

_____

Plant Notes _____

_____

_____

_____

Tree Notes _____

_____

_____

_____

Yard Notes _____

_____

_____

_____

Visitors _____

_____

_____

February

WEEK 3

Weather • Hours of Sun

_____

_____

_____

_____

In Bloom

_____

_____

_____

_____

Plant Notes

_____

_____

_____

_____

Tree Notes

_____

_____

_____

_____

Yard Notes

_____

_____

_____

Visitors

_____

_____

_____

February

WEEK 4-5

Weather • Hours of Sun

_____

_____

_____

_____

In Bloom

_____

_____

_____

_____

Plant Notes

_____

_____

_____

_____

Tree Notes

_____

_____

_____

_____

Yard Notes

_____

_____

_____

_____

Visitors

_____

_____

_____

General Thoughts, Observations, & Sketches

TIPS AND REMINDERS

THE TIMING FOR THESE EVENTS WILL DEPEND ON LATITUDE.

- As you carry out your early spring cleanup chores, create a brush pile with fallen branches as a shelter for wildlife.

- Inventory your garage and garden shed and mark for safe disposal substances too toxic to use. Find out your community's chemical disposal day schedule and location.

- Research the life cycles of insect pests so that you'll be prepared to use alternatives to pesticides.

- Add compost to planting beds. Sow seeds of summer annuals indoors, remembering to pick species used by butterflies and hummingbirds.

- Clean out and repair nest boxes.

March

General Thoughts, Observations, & Sketches

March
Week 1

Weather • Hours of Sun _____

_____

_____

_____

_____

In Bloom _____

_____

_____

_____

_____

Plant Notes _____

_____

_____

_____

_____

Tree Notes _____

_____

_____

_____

_____

Yard Notes _____

_____

_____

_____

Visitors _____

_____

_____

_____

March

WEEK 2

Weather • Hours of Sun

_____
_____
_____
_____

In Bloom

_____
_____
_____
_____

Plant Notes

_____
_____
_____
_____

Tree Notes

_____
_____
_____

Yard Notes

_____
_____
_____
_____

Visitors

_____
_____
_____

March
WEEK 3

Weather • Hours of Sun

In Bloom

Plant Notes

Tree Notes

Yard Notes

Visitors

March
WEEK 4-5

Weather • Hours of Sun

In Bloom

Plant Notes

Tree Notes

Yard Notes

Visitors

TIPS AND REMINDERS

THE TIMING FOR THESE EVENTS WILL DEPEND ON LATITUDE.

* Prepare for spring warbler migration: Listen to audio recordings of the birds to brush up on their calls. Review a field guide to remember what to look for and when.

* Set your lawn mower height to three inches or higher to promote healthy growth. Remove the clippings box and let your clippings act as a mulch for your lawn.

* Celebrate John James Audubon's birthday, April 26, by planting a native tree or shrub beneficial to birds.

* Fill your hummingbird feeders. The jewels will soon arrive. Dissolve one part sugar into four parts boiling water. Cool the mixture before setting it out for the birds.

April
General Thoughts, Observations, & Sketches

April
WEEK 1

Weather • Hours of Sun

_____

_____

_____

_____

In Bloom

_____

_____

_____

_____

Plant Notes

_____

_____

_____

Tree Notes

_____

_____

_____

_____

Yard Notes

_____

_____

_____

Visitors

_____

_____

_____

April

WEEK 2

Weather • Hours of Sun

In Bloom

Plant Notes

Tree Notes

Yard Notes

Visitors

April

WEEK 3

Weather • Hours of Sun _____

_____

_____

_____

In Bloom _____

_____

_____

_____

Plant Notes _____

_____

_____

_____

Tree Notes _____

_____

_____

_____

Yard Notes _____

_____

_____

_____

Visitors _____

_____

_____

_____

April
WEEK 4-5

Weather • *Hours of Sun*

In Bloom

Plant Notes

Tree Notes

Yard Notes

Visitors

Tips and Reminders

The timing for these events will depend on latitude.

❀ When preparing your garden, don't forget to plant late-blooming nectar plants for migrating monarch butterflies.

❀ Make sure all your data for Project FeederWatch has been submitted (birds.cornell.edu/PFW/).

❀ Create a butterfly/hummingbird garden.

❤ Install a water drip or fountain mist to attract birds to your birdbath.

❀ Research the name of a local wildlife rehabilitator to have on hand in case you see injured or orphaned birds during the upcoming busy breeding season.

❀ Seek out and attend local plant sales conducted by native plant societies or nurseries.

May

General Thoughts, Observations, & Sketches

May
WEEK 1

Weather • Hours of Sun

_____

_____

_____

_____

In Bloom

_____

_____

_____

_____

Plant Notes

_____

_____

_____

_____

Tree Notes

_____

_____

_____

_____

Yard Notes

_____

_____

_____

_____

Visitors

_____

_____

_____

May

WEEK 2

Weather • Hours of Sun

In Bloom

Plant Notes

Tree Notes

Yard Notes

Visitors

May
WEEK 3

Weather • Hours of Sun

_____

_____

_____

_____

In Bloom

_____

_____

_____

_____

Plant Notes

_____

_____

_____

_____

Tree Notes

_____

_____

_____

_____

Yard Notes

_____

_____

_____

_____

Visitors

_____

_____

_____

May

WEEK 4-5

Weather • Hours of Sun

_____

_____

_____

_____

In Bloom

_____

_____

_____

_____

Plant Notes

_____

_____

_____

_____

Tree Notes

_____

_____

_____

_____

Yard Notes

_____

_____

_____

Visitors

_____

_____

_____

THE TIMING FOR THESE EVENTS WILL DEPEND ON LATITUDE.

- Nesting season is in full swing. Continue to keep your cat indoors!

- Take part in a nesting bird observation or monitoring project, such as the Breeding Bird Survey (www.pwrc.usgs.gov/bbs/) or the Birdhouse Network (www.birds.cornell.edu/birdhouse/).

- If you haven't already done so, build a compost pile with grass clippings, kitchen scraps, and leaf litter.

- Change the water in your birdbath regularly and keep it filled.

- Scout your habitat frequently to detect pest problems early, when control methods are most effective. Remember to tolerate some damage.

June

General Thoughts, Observations, & Sketches

June
WEEK 1

Weather • Hours of Sun

In Bloom

Plant Notes

Tree Notes

Yard Notes

Visitors

June
WEEK 2

Weather • Hours of Sun

_____

In Bloom

_____

Plant Notes

_____

Tree Notes

_____

Yard Notes

_____

Visitors

_____

June
WEEK 3

Weather • Hours of Sun

_____

_____

_____

_____

In Bloom

_____

_____

_____

_____

Plant Notes

_____

_____

_____

_____

Tree Notes

_____

_____

_____

_____

Yard Notes

_____

_____

_____

Visitors

_____

_____

_____

June
WEEK 4-5

Weather • Hours of Sun

In Bloom

Plant Notes

Tree Notes

Yard Notes

Visitors

THE TIMING FOR THESE EVENTS WILL DEPEND ON LATITUDE.

- Mulch garden beds to conserve moisture and control weeds.

- While the yard is in full bloom, take notes and photographs and make sketches to remember what looks good and which areas need additional plants and habitat restoration.

- Continue to monitor your yard for insect pests and use the least-toxic treatment methods possible.

- Install drip irrigation in case of long dry periods.

- Remember to leave nitrogen-rich grass clippings on the lawn after mowing.

July

General Thoughts, Observations, & Sketches

July
WEEK 1

Weather • Hours of Sun

In Bloom

Plant Notes

Tree Notes

Yard Notes

Visitors

July
WEEK 2

Weather • Hours of Sun

_____

_____

_____

_____

In Bloom

_____

_____

_____

_____

Plant Notes

_____

_____

_____

_____

Tree Notes

_____

_____

_____

_____

Yard Notes

_____

_____

_____

_____

Visitors

_____

_____

_____

July

WEEK 3

Weather • Hours of Sun

_____

_____

_____

_____

In Bloom

_____

_____

_____

_____

Plant Notes

_____

_____

_____

_____

Tree Notes

_____

_____

_____

_____

Yard Notes

_____

_____

_____

_____

Visitors

_____

_____

_____

_____

July
WEEK 4-5

Weather • Hours of Sun

In Bloom

Plant Notes

Tree Notes

Yard Notes

Visitors

THE TIMING FOR THESE EVENTS WILL DEPEND ON LATITUDE.

- Collect your native wildflower seeds as soon as they are ripe. Store them in a paper bag in a cool place.

- Assess the areas in your yard that may need additional plants.

- Prepare a landscape plan for the planting of trees and shrubs in the fall.

- After the last broods of the season have fledged, clean out all your birdhouses, removing old nests.

- Prepare your bird feeders for the migration season. Clean them well.

August

General Thoughts, Observations, & Sketches

August
WEEK 1

Weather • Hours of Sun

In Bloom

Plant Notes

Tree Notes

Yard Notes

Visitors

August
WEEK 2

Weather • Hours of Sun

_____

_____

_____

_____

In Bloom

_____

_____

_____

_____

Plant Notes

_____

_____

_____

_____

Tree Notes

_____

_____

_____

_____

Yard Notes

_____

_____

_____

_____

Visitors

_____

_____

_____

_____

August
WEEK 3

Weather • Hours of Sun _____

_____

_____

_____

In Bloom _____

_____

_____

_____

Plant Notes _____

_____

_____

_____

Tree Notes _____

_____

_____

_____

Yard Notes _____

_____

_____

_____

Visitors _____

_____

_____

August
WEEK 4-5

Weather • Hours of Sun

_____

_____

_____

In Bloom

_____

_____

_____

Plant Notes

_____

_____

_____

Tree Notes

_____

_____

_____

Yard Notes

_____

_____

_____

Visitors

_____

_____

The timing for these events will depend on latitude.

- Fill your bird feeders. Summer residents need to fatten up before they head south, other migrants will be passing through, and winter residents will recognize the welcome mat and stick around.

- While the weather is still comfortable, install netting, such as fruit-tree netting, in front of windows near feeders to prevent birds from crashing into the window.

- Set up roosting boxes to provide shelter for birds during the winter.

- Remove old bird nests and scrape clean so that birds can use boxes or winter roosts.

- Divide and transplant early-blooming perennials.

- Take a soil sample and send it to your local cooperative extension to determine pH and nutrient levels. If amendments are needed, fall is the best time to apply them.

September

General Thoughts, Observations, & Sketches

General Thoughts, Observations, & Sketches

September
Week 1

Weather • Hours of Sun

_____
_____
_____
_____

In Bloom

_____
_____
_____
_____

Plant Notes

_____
_____
_____
_____

Tree Notes

_____
_____
_____
_____

Yard Notes

_____
_____
_____
_____

Visitors

_____
_____
_____

September

WEEK 2

Weather • Hours of Sun

_____

_____

_____

_____

In Bloom

_____

_____

_____

_____

Plant Notes

_____

_____

_____

_____

Tree Notes

_____

_____

_____

_____

Yard Notes

_____

_____

_____

Visitors

_____

_____

_____

September
WEEK 3

Weather • Hours of Sun

_____

_____

_____

_____

In Bloom

_____

_____

_____

_____

Plant Notes

_____

_____

_____

_____

Tree Notes

_____

_____

_____

_____

Yard Notes

_____

_____

_____

_____

Visitors

_____

_____

_____

September
WEEK 4-5

Weather • Hours of Sun

_____

_____

_____

_____

In Bloom

_____

_____

_____

_____

Plant Notes

_____

_____

_____

_____

Tree Notes

_____

_____

_____

_____

Yard Notes

_____

_____

_____

_____

Visitors

_____

_____

_____

THE TIMING FOR THESE EVENTS WILL DEPEND ON LATITUDE.

- Stock up on bird seed and suet for the winter months. Patronize your local Audubon chapter's seed sale.

- Keep your hummingbird feeders full until two weeks after the last migrant has left.

- Enjoy migration by going to a local hawk watch. Check your Audubon chapter or Audubon center to find out the nearest site.

- Rake fallen leaves under shrubs and into garden beds as a protective mulch layer and as foraging areas for birds. Or, shred fallen leaves with a mower and let them remain on the lawn as mulch. Another option is to simply place collected leaves into your compost along with other garden debris.

- Create a brush pile from fallen branches.

- Leave certain garden cleanup chores for the spring. Remove rotted debris to prevent the harboring of pests and diseases, but allow spent grasses and other seed-bearing plants to remain standing throughout the winter as a food source for the birds.

- Add organic matter to the soil by tilling in summer mulch and adding compost or manure.

October

General Thoughts, Observations, & Sketches

October
WEEK 1

Weather • Hours of Sun

In Bloom

Plant Notes

Tree Notes

Yard Notes

Visitors

October
WEEK 2

Weather • Hours of Sun

_____

_____

_____

_____

In Bloom

_____

_____

_____

_____

Plant Notes

_____

_____

_____

_____

Tree Notes

_____

_____

_____

_____

Yard Notes

_____

_____

_____

_____

Visitors

_____

_____

_____

_____

October
WEEK 3

Weather • Hours of Sun

_____

_____

_____

_____

In Bloom

_____

_____

_____

_____

Plant Notes

_____

_____

_____

_____

Tree Notes

_____

_____

_____

_____

Yard Notes

_____

_____

_____

_____

Visitors

_____

_____

_____

October

WEEK 4-5

Weather • Hours of Sun

In Bloom

Plant Notes

Tree Notes

Yard Notes

Visitors

THE TIMING FOR THESE EVENTS WILL DEPEND ON LATITUDE.

- Sign up for Project FeederWatch (www.birds.cornell.edu/PFW/) and become a citizen scientist by counting the birds that come to your feeding station from November to April.

- Plant deciduous trees and shrubs up until the ground freezes.

- Set up a submersible heater in your birdbath to keep water unfrozen and accessible throughout the winter.

- Clean and oil your garden tools for winter storage.

- Begin sowing seeds that need stratification or cold treatment.

November
General Thoughts, Observations, & Sketches

General Thoughts, Observations, & Sketches

November

WEEK 1

Weather • Hours of Sun

_____

_____

_____

_____

In Bloom

_____

_____

_____

Plant Notes

_____

_____

_____

_____

Tree Notes

_____

_____

_____

_____

Yard Notes

_____

_____

_____

_____

Visitors

_____

_____

_____

November

WEEK 2

Weather • Hours of Sun _____

_____

_____

In Bloom _____

_____

_____

Plant Notes _____

_____

_____

Tree Notes _____

_____

_____

Yard Notes _____

_____

_____

Visitors _____

_____

_____

November

WEEK 3

Weather • Hours of Sun

In Bloom

Plant Notes

Tree Notes

Yard Notes

Visitors

November

WEEK 4-5

Weather • Hours of Sun _____
_____
_____
_____

In Bloom _____
_____
_____
_____

Plant Notes _____
_____
_____
_____

Tree Notes _____
_____
_____
_____

Yard Notes _____
_____
_____
_____

Visitors _____
_____
_____

THE TIMING FOR THESE EVENTS WILL DEPEND ON LATITUDE.

* Participate in Audubon's Christmas Bird Count (www.audubon.org/bird/cbc/index.html).

* Decorate the trees and shrubs in your yard with holiday treats for the birds. Make an edible garland for birds by stringing popcorn, whole peanuts, cranberries, and raisins. Insert peanut butter into crevices in large pine cones and hang these from trees.

* After the ground freezes, mulch around perennial beds to prevent heaving during freeze/thaw cycles.

* Before the ground freezes, erect nest boxes for next spring. Bluebirds, especially, will check out possible nesting sites in late winter.

December

General Thoughts, Observations, & Sketches

December

WEEK 1

Weather • Hours of Sun
_____

_____
_____
_____

In Bloom _____

_____
_____
_____

Plant Notes _____

_____
_____
_____

Tree Notes _____

_____
_____
_____

Yard Notes _____

_____
_____
_____

Visitors _____

_____
_____
_____

December

WEEK 2

Weather • Hours of Sun

_____

_____

_____

_____

In Bloom

_____

_____

_____

_____

Plant Notes

_____

_____

_____

_____

Tree Notes

_____

_____

_____

_____

Yard Notes

_____

_____

_____

_____

Visitors

_____

_____

_____

December

WEEK 3

Weather • Hours of Sun

_____

_____

_____

_____

In Bloom

_____

_____

_____

_____

Plant Notes

_____

_____

_____

_____

Tree Notes

_____

_____

_____

_____

Yard Notes

_____

_____

_____

_____

Visitors

_____

_____

_____

December
WEEK 4-5

Weather • Hours of Sun

In Bloom

Plant Notes

Tree Notes

Yard Notes

Visitors

Audubon At Home, "Keeping Wildlife Safe"
www.audubon.org/bird/at_home/KeepWildlifeSafe.html

Audubon At Home, "Safe Bird Feeding"
www.audubon.org/bird/at_home/bird_feeding/index.html

Stephen W. Kress, "The Winter Banquet," *Audubon* **magazine, Jan/Feb 2000**
magazine.audubon.org/backyard/backyard0001.html

Cornell Lab of Ornithology, Project FeederWatch
www.birds.cornell.edu/PFW/

US Fish and Wildlife Service, "Backyard Bird Feeding"
training.fws.gov/library/Bird_Publications/feed.html
For a print copy, call 800-344-WILD (344-9453).

Birdhouses and Shelters

US Fish and Wildlife Service, "Homes for Birds"
library.fws.gov/Bird_Publications/house.html
For a print copy, call 800-344-WILD (344-9453).

Audubon Resource Page
www.audubon.org/educate/expert/birdhouse.html

Cornell Lab of Ornithology, "Birdhouse Basics"
www.birds.cornell.edu/birdhouse/bhbasics/refrchart.html

Protective Cover for Birds

USDA Natural Resources Conservation Service, "Backyard Conservation Tip Sheet on Providing Shelter for Wildlife"
>   www.nrcs.usda.gov/feature/backyard/sheltwild.html
>   For a print copy, call 888-LANDCARE (526-3227).

More About the Needs of Birds

U.S. Fish and Wildlife Service, "For the Birds" online pamphlets
>   migratorybirds.fws.gov/pamphlet/pamplets.html
>   A print booklet consolidating most of this material is available for $1.00; call 888-8 PUEBLO (878-3256) and ask for publication 351M.

How to Build a Pond or Wetland

USDA Natural Resources Conservation Service, "Backyard Conservation Tip Sheet: Backyard Ponds"
>   www.nrcs.usda.gov/feature/backyard/BkPond.html
>   For a print copy, call 888-LANDCARE (526-3227).

John Manuel, "Homegrown Wetlands," *Audubon* magazine, Jul/Aug 1999
>   magazine.audubon.org/backyard/backyard9807.html

Suggested below are a number of actions you can take to incorporate native plants into your landscape. Check off each as you complete it. Set a target date for accomplishing all of the recommended activities.

1. LEARN how native species are defined. There are a number of definitions in use. Is it a plant historically found in your immediate region? Or one that is indigenous to your state? Or is it any plant that occurred in North America before European settlement? Choose your operational definition. This will help you select the plants you want in your habitat.

2. FAMILIARIZE yourself with plants considered native to your area. Which ones may have been on the site where you now live? Contact local parks and arboreta, your local Audubon chapter or center, or your local native plant society for guidance. Take a hike in nearby natural areas to see native plants in their habitat.

3. DEVISE a plan before you plant. Develop a map that shows elements of your property, such as structures and hardscapes (house, patio, paths), sunny/shady areas, wet/dry areas, soil quality, etc. Choose a site on which to begin to incorporate native plantings. Is it in shade and suitable to a woodland garden? Is it in full sun, calling for a butterfly garden? Is it constantly moist, calling for wetland plants? Remember that placing the proper plant in the proper site is a key to success.

4. PREPARE the site. Loosen soil with shovels, garden fork, or tiller. Add several inches of compost. Or, you may want to minimize soil disturbance to keep weed seeds dormant and instead cover the site with a thick layer of mulch. Layers of black-and-white printed newspapers, at least five sheets thick, work well to prevent the sunlight from reaching the soil. Spread compost on top of the newspapers to create a planting bed. Soil organisms will eventually decompose the paper.

5. SELECT the plants you would like in your habitat. You can simply pick the species you enjoy, or you can choose them according to the wildlife you'd like to attract. For instance, if you want to lure monarch butterflies, you would select milkweed, which is the only plant monarch larvae feed upon. Create a plant community with plants of varying growth habits and sizes. Make a list that you can take with you to nurseries or refer to while catalog shopping.

6. FIND sources for the plants you choose. When you purchase plants, make sure they have been propagated at a nursery and not dug up from the wild. Many native grasses and meadow plants are germinated from seeds. Collect catalogs of native plant and seed suppliers, and check your local nurseries to see if they sell the native plants you've selected.

7. BEGIN planting! Monitor soil moisture to ensure success of young plants. Remove invasive weeds that will aggressively compete for water and nutrients. Tolerate some insect damage. Gently dissuade hungry herbivores (rabbits, deer, etc.) from eating young plants. Once seedlings are established, pull up a chair and watch them grow!

RESOURCES/LINKS

US Department of Transportation/Federal Highway Administration, Roadside Use of Native Plants

Parts of this handbook (Island Press, 2000) are available online; see in particular "What Is a Native Plant?" by L. E. Morse, J. M. Swearingen, and J. M. Randall

www.fhwa.dot.gov/environment/rdsduse/rdsduse5.htm

USDA Natural Resources Conservation Service, Native Plants and Gardening Links

List of resources including native gardens, seed sources, and much more

plants.usda.gov/links.html

North American Native Plant Society

List of native plant resources and organizations

www.nanps.org

US Environmental Protection Agency, "Landscaping with Native Plants Factsheet"

Excellent compendium of native plant information and resources

www.epa.gov/greenacres/nativeplants/factsht.html

Audubon At Home in Seattle, "Gardening for Life: An Inspirational Guide to Creating Healthy Habitat"

See Chapter 3 of this downloadable booklet for step-by-step instructions on creating healthy backyard habitat, including how to draw a base map of your property, designing a garden layout, and developing a planting plan

www.audubon.org/bird/at_home/GardeningForLife.html

Lady Bird Johnson Wildflower Center

Austin, Texas–based center; website includes image gallery and native plants database

www.wildflower.org

Suggested below are a number of actions you can take to protect water quality. They are in no particular order—focus initially on those that are easiest for you to accomplish. Check off each as you complete it or incorporate it into your land-care routines. Set a target date for accomplishing all of the recommended activities.

IDENTIFY your watershed. Learn where the water that drains off your property goes. Which rivers, streams, lakes, or other water bodies are affected by your actions?

TEST your soil before applying fertilizers or other nutrients to avoid overapplication.

REDUCE pesticide use. Pesticides can contaminate water through surface runoff into streams and lakes and by leaching into groundwater. Take stock of your pesticide use and see where you can make changes. On lawns, explore nontoxic alternatives and aim to eliminate pesticides that are used for aesthetic purposes only.

PATCH bare soil areas in your yard to prevent erosion and runoff. If the exposed spot is within your lawn, choose a native grass or groundcover. If it's under a tree in heavy shade where nothing will grow, mulch the area to avoid compaction.

SWEEP, rather than hose down, sidewalks, driveways, and other impervious surfaces.

USE a funnel for pouring when filling your lawn mower or other gasoline-powered tools. The EPA reports that tens of millions of gallons of gasoline are spilled each year while refueling garden equipment.

DISPOSE of pet waste in the garbage—not in the street or where it can be carried away by precipitation.

MANAGE landscape projects properly. Disturbed soil is susceptible to runoff during planting, and during installation of irrigation systems, patios, paths, or other landscape elements. Schedule work during dry-weather seasons and replant as soon as possible to prevent erosion. Shovel construction residue into the garbage; do not wash it down the storm drain.

MINIMIZE lawn area and implement healthy lawn care practices. Large lawns with non-native grasses consume overdoses of pesticides, fertilizers, and water, which can contribute to contaminated runoff. Initiate the effort by expanding a garden border and letting the grass grow to at least three inches before you mow.

REPLACE paved surfaces, such as a garden path or driveway, with porous material. Choose an area to be replaced with a substitute material. Native grasses and groundcovers, mulch, gravel, brick, and sustainable wood decking are some alternatives that allow rainwater to seep into the ground. Begin small and expand.

USE rainwater to your advantage. Collect or divert runoff from your roof and create a rain garden. Direct the runoff from your roof to a low spot in your yard planted with native wetland plants, allowing the water to seep into the ground rather than stream down your driveway, picking up pollutants on the way.

MAINTAIN a natural buffer zone between your landscaped area and any ponds or streams to prevent bank erosion and to filter contaminants. Allow the native vegetation to grow high or plant with native water-loving species.

AVOID planting trees too close to septic systems. The roots can crack pipes and cause wastewater seepage.

RESOURCES/LINKS

US Environmental Protection Agency, Watershed Information Network
Tools to identify your watershed and resources to help you protect it
www.epa.gov/win/

US Environmental Protection Agency, Polluted Runoff (Nonpoint Source Pollution)
Information and resources for reducing nonpoint source pollution
www.epa.gov/owow/nps/whatis.html

Cornell Cooperative Extension, "The Homeowner's Lawn Care Water Quality Almanac"
Learn how to take care of your lawn without contributing to pollution of your watershed
www.gardening.cornell.edu/lawn/almanac/index.html

USDA Natural Resources Conservation Service, "Backyard Conservation Tip Sheet: Nutrient Management"
Tips on soil testing and proper application of fertilizer and other soil amendments
www.nrcs.usda.gov/feature/backyard/NutMgt.html
For a print copy, call 888-LANDCARE (526-3227).

Audubon At Home, "Reduce Pesticides!"
Online resources for responsible pesticide use
www.audubon.org/bird/at_home/reduce_pesticides.html

Janet Marinelli, "Good to the Last Drop," *Audubon* **magazine, Sep 2003**
magazine.audubon.org/backyard/backyard0309.html#raingarden

Suggested below are a number of actions you can take to reduce your use of pesticides with the ultimate goal of eliminating them completely.

Check off each as you complete it or incorporate it into your land care routines. Set a target date for accomplishing all of the recommended activities.

1. **ASSESS your use of pesticides.** How often do you use them and for what purpose? Do you use an herbicide to remove weeds from your lawn? Do you use an insecticide to get rid of slugs in your garden? Do you apply a fungicide to combat black spot on your roses?

List the pesticides you use, the "pest" you are targeting with each, and your frequency of use. Be sure to include those pesticides that are applied by any lawn care or pest control professionals you hire.

2. **QUESTION yourself.** Think about why you turn to chemicals—is it because you know of no other methods? Do you really have a "pest" or just a minor irritant? How severe is the problem—a few leaves or the entire plant? Do you have a spider or two, or an infestation of roaches? Can the "problem" be overlooked? Chart the answers to these questions for each pesticide you've listed in #1 above and see where you can immediately decrease the amount and frequency of pesticide applications, or eliminate them altogether.

3. **INVENTORY the pesticide products you have on hand.** Safely discard those that you've identified in #2 as being unnecessary, as well as any products that are poorly labeled or discontinued. Contact local solid waste management or health agencies for disposal guidelines. State

and local laws may dictate stricter guidelines than those provided on the label.

4. RESEARCH alternatives for those pesticides you've identified as still being needed. The aim is to use the least toxic method possible or eliminate pesticides completely. Visit our "You Have a Choice!" web pages to identify your options (www.audubon.org/bird/at_home/alternatives.html). Pick at least one option and give it a try. As you find success, cross the pesticide you'll no longer need off your list and safely discard any remaining product.

5. PRACTICE prevention. Pests are usually a symptom rather than a source of a problem. Prevent problems that can lead to pest infestations by incorporating the following activities into your land care routines:

• Remove pest hiding and breeding sites—inside and out. Remove trash and standing water from outdoor areas. Keep indoor areas clean and dry.

• Maintain healthy soil with the help of compost. Healthy soil contains beneficial organisms that keep disease and pests in check. Healthy soil also breeds healthy plants, which resist disease and are less likely to succumb to pests. This week, start collecting kitchen and yard waste and begin a compost pile.

• Grow the right plant in the right spot. Take stock of the plants in your yard; if they are not in the appropriate place, transplant them to a more favorable site. For instance, if the plant needs sun, put it where it will receive the right amount of light. If it likes wet conditions, plant it near water. If it's an acid-loving plant, make sure the soil's pH is appropriate. The stronger the plant, the less susceptible it will be to disease and pests.

• Plant native species. They are more resistant to pest problems because they have evolved under local environmental conditions. Explore ways to begin incorporating natives into your yard. Start by adding one or two native plants to your existing gardens.

• Make natural pest enemies welcome. Toads, dragonflies, nematodes, bats, and numerous species of birds and other insects are your natural allies in pest control. Learn who they are and support them.

• Monitor your outdoor space regularly and look for early warning signs of problems. Determine whether damage was the result of insects, disease, nutrient imbalance, or misapplication of chemicals. Take the time to identify suspected pests and the reason for their presence: Was the fungus a result of poor watering habits, or was the insect issue due to a plant weakened by poor soil? Correct the source of the problem rather than resorting to pesticides.

RESOURCES/LINKS

Audubon At Home, "Healthier Choices: A Guide to Healthier Pest Control"

www.audubon.org/bird/at_home/pdf/HealthierChoices.pdf

Audubon At Home, "Reduce Pesticides!"
Online resources for responsible pesticide use

www.audubon.org/bird/at_home/reduce_pesticides.html

Home and Garden Information Center, University of Maryland/Maryland Cooperative Extension, "IPM (Integrated Pest Management): A Common Sense Approach to Managing Problems in Your Landscape"
> w.montgomerycountymd.gov/mc/services/dep/Grasscycling/commonsense.pdf

PAN (Pesticide Action Network) Pesticide Database
Extensive toxicity and regulatory information for pesticides, including searchable databases of pesticide products, pesticide alternatives, and more
> www.pesticideinfo.org/index.html

Earth 911
Search by zip code to find hazardous waste disposal sites and other home and community conservation resources
> www.earth911.org/master.asp

USDA Natural Resources Conservation Service, "Backyard Conservation Tip Sheet: Composting"
> www.nrcs.usda.gov/feature/backyard/Compost.html
> For a print copy, call 888-LANDCARE (526-3227).

Cornell University, "Biological Control: A Guide to Natural Enemies in North America"
> www.nysaes.cornell.edu/ent/biocontrol/

Suppliers

NAME

ADDRESS

WEBSITE

NAME

ADDRESS

☎

WEBSITE

NAME

ADDRESS

☎

WEBSITE

NAME

ADDRESS

☎

WEBSITE

NAME

ADDRESS

☎

WEBSITE

NAME

ADDRESS

☎

WEBSITE

NAME

ADDRESS

☎

WEBSITE

NAME

ADDRESS

☎

WEBSITE

NAME

ADDRESS

☎

WEBSITE

NAME

ADDRESS

☎

WEBSITE

NAME

ADDRESS

☎

WEBSITE

NAME

ADDRESS

☎

WEBSITE

NAME

ADDRESS

☎

WEBSITE

NAME

ADDRESS

☎

WEBSITE

NAME

ADDRESS

☎

WEBSITE

NAME

ADDRESS

☎

WEBSITE

NAME

ADDRESS

☎

WEBSITE

NAME

ADDRESS

☎

WEBSITE

NAME

ADDRESS

☎

WEBSITE

NAME

ADDRESS

☎

WEBSITE

NAME

ADDRESS

☎

WEBSITE

NAME

ADDRESS

☎

WEBSITE

NAME

ADDRESS

☎

WEBSITE

NAME

ADDRESS

☎

WEBSITE

NAME

ADDRESS

☎

WEBSITE

NAME

ADDRESS

☎

WEBSITE

NAME

ADDRESS

☎

WEBSITE

NAME

ADDRESS

☎

WEBSITE

NAME

ADDRESS

☎

WEBSITE

NAME

ADDRESS

☎

WEBSITE

NAME

ADDRESS

☎

WEBSITE

NAME

ADDRESS

☎

WEBSITE

NAME

ADDRESS

☎

WEBSITE

NAME

ADDRESS

☎

WEBSITE

NAME

ADDRESS

☎

WEBSITE

COMMON NAME

SCIENTIFIC NAME

NOTES:

COMMON: SCIENTIFIC:

NOTES:

COMMON: SCIENTIFIC:

NOTES:

COMMON: SCIENTIFIC:

NOTES:

COMMON: SCIENTIFIC:

NOTES:

COMMON: SCIENTIFIC:

NOTES:

COMMON: SCIENTIFIC:

NOTES:

COMMON: SCIENTIFIC:

NOTES:

COMMON: SCIENTIFIC:

NOTES:

COMMON: SCIENTIFIC:

NOTES:

COMMON: SCIENTIFIC:

NOTES:

COMMON: SCIENTIFIC:

NOTES:

Plant List

COMMON NAME   SCIENTIFIC NAME

NOTES:

COMMON: SCIENTIFIC:

NOTES:

COMMON: SCIENTIFIC:

NOTES:

COMMON: SCIENTIFIC:

NOTES:

COMMON: SCIENTIFIC:

NOTES:

COMMON: SCIENTIFIC:

NOTES:

COMMON: SCIENTIFIC:

NOTES:

COMMON: SCIENTIFIC:

NOTES:

COMMON: SCIENTIFIC:

NOTES:

COMMON: SCIENTIFIC:

NOTES:

COMMON: SCIENTIFIC:

NOTES:

COMMON NAME

SCIENTIFIC NAME

_____

NOTES: _____

COMMON: _____ SCIENTIFIC: _____

NOTES: _____

COMMON: _____ SCIENTIFIC: _____

NOTES: _____

COMMON: _____ SCIENTIFIC: _____

NOTES: _____

COMMON: _____ SCIENTIFIC: _____

NOTES: _____

COMMON: _____ SCIENTIFIC: _____

NOTES: _____

COMMON: _____ SCIENTIFIC: _____

NOTES: _____

COMMON: _____ SCIENTIFIC: _____

NOTES: _____

COMMON: _____ SCIENTIFIC: _____

NOTES: _____

COMMON: _____ SCIENTIFIC: _____

NOTES: _____

COMMON: _____ SCIENTIFIC: _____

NOTES: _____

COMMON: _____ SCIENTIFIC: _____

NOTES: _____

_____

Plant List

COMMON NAME   SCIENTIFIC NAME

_____   _____

NOTES: _____

COMMON: _____   SCIENTIFIC: _____

NOTES: _____

COMMON: _____   SCIENTIFIC: _____

NOTES: _____

COMMON: _____   SCIENTIFIC: _____

NOTES: _____

COMMON: _____   SCIENTIFIC: _____

NOTES: _____

COMMON: _____   SCIENTIFIC: _____

NOTES: _____

COMMON: _____   SCIENTIFIC: _____

NOTES: _____

COMMON: _____   SCIENTIFIC: _____

NOTES: _____

COMMON: _____   SCIENTIFIC: _____

NOTES: _____

COMMON: _____   SCIENTIFIC: _____

NOTES: _____

COMMON: _____   SCIENTIFIC: _____

NOTES: _____

_____

USDA Plant Hardiness Zone Map

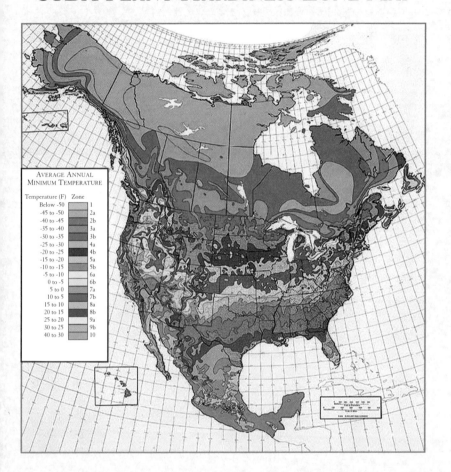

Average Annual Minimum Temperature

Temperature (F)	Zone
Below -50	1
-45 to -50	2a
-40 to -45	2b
-35 to -40	3a
-30 to -35	3b
-25 to -30	4a
-20 to -25	4b
-15 to -20	5a
-10 to -15	5b
-5 to -10	6a
0 to -5	6b
5 to 0	7a
10 to 5	7b
15 to 10	8a
20 to 15	8b
25 to 20	9a
30 to 25	9b
40 to 30	10

A gift to Audubon will bring you . . .

- Membership in the National Audubon Society

- A full year of *Audubon* magazine, filled with magnificent nature photography, insight, information, and inspiration

- Membership in your local Audubon chapter (if there is one in your area), with the opportunity to participate in exciting programs and special events

- Special invitations to explore Audubon Centers and participate in Audubon workshops and camps

- Travel opportunities with Audubon's Nature Odysseys

- The satisfaction of knowing that your gift helps support sanctuaries, field research, environmental educational programs, public policy advocacy, and other efforts critical to the protection of wildlife and their habitats

Please make checks payable to the National Audubon Society. Allow four to six weeks for delivery of magazine. Mail the membership form to:

National Audubon Society
Membership Data Center
PO Box 52529
Boulder CO 80322-2529

MEMBERSHIP FORM

☐ Yes, you can count on me to help protect America's birds, wildlife, and their vital habitats.

Enclosed is my gift of:

☐ $20   ☐ $30   ☐ $50   ☐ $100   ☐ Other ____

☐ Check enclosed   ☐ Please bill me

NAME _____

ADDRESS _____

CITY _____   STATE _____   ZIP _____

Your gift to Audubon is tax deductible except for the $15 fair market value of *Audubon* magazine.